TORRE DE BELÉM

TORRE DE BELÉM

PAULO PEREIRA

Ministério da Cultura

ippar

Instituto Português do
Património Arquitectónico

This edition copyright © Instituto Português do Património Arquitectónico (IPPAR)
and Scala Publishers Ltd 2005

First published in 2005 by
Scala Publishers Ltd
Northburgh House,
10 Northburgh Street
London EC1V 0AT

Author: Paulo Pereira
Editorial coordination (DE/IPPAR): Manuel Lacardo, Miguel Soromenho
Editorial coordination (Scala Publishers): Jessica Hodge, Oliver Craske,
    Emma Pattison, Katy Moran
Picture research and iconography: Dulce de Freitas Ferraz (DCD/IPPAR)
Designed by Anikst Design
Translated from the Portuguese by Gilla Evans
Index by Diana LeCore

Plans: © IPPAR/Maria João Saldanha

Printed and bound in Spain

10 9 8 7 6 5 4 3 2 1

ISBN: 1 85759 311 1

All photographs by Luis Pavão with contribution from Carlos Sá
Except: IPPAR/Henrique Ruas (cover, pages 2, 14, 33 right, 34 left, 37, 38 left, 55
right), IPPAR/Manuel Ribeiro (page 41), Alexander Braz Mimoso (page 59),
Photographic Reproduction of the Municipal Photographic Archive of
Lisbon C.M.L. (pages 56, 57, 58)

Acknowledgements:
The author would like to thank all the organisations which have provided material
and pictures for this edition, and the staff of the Jerónimos Monastery. With special
thanks to the staff of the Research Department, to Drª Dulce Ferraz, Henrique Ruas
(IPPAR) and photographer Luis Pavão who has once again lent his magnificent and
consistent artistic vision to this book.

CONTENTS

A Drawbridge
B Nave of the bastion
C Cloister

-1 Underground floor
0 Nave of the bastion
1 Terrace of the bastion
2 First room or "Governor's Room"
3 Second room or "Kings' Room"
4 Third room or "Assembly Room"
5 Fourth room or "Chapel"
6 Terrace of the Torre

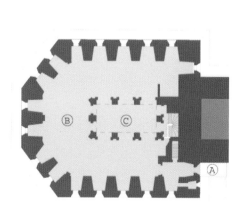

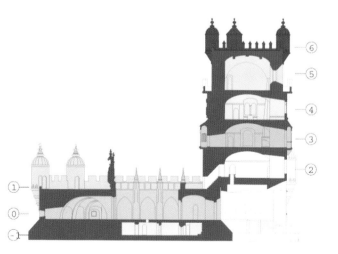

FOREWORD

Its extraordinary location on the riverbank of what was once Restelo beach, its singular architecture, which some see as an echo of the exotic styles of the Maghreb or the Orient, or even its obvious symbolic value, linked as it is to the adventure of the Portuguese Discoveries and Vasco da Gama's first voyage to India, make the Torre de Belém one of the most emblematic examples of Portugal's architectural heritage and one of the most important buildings under the protection of the Instituto Português do Património Arquitectónico (IPPAR).

The many thousands of visitors who come here each year take away the impression of a tower still medieval in form but already open to the more cosmopolitan influences of the Renaissance, and are able to see its position within a majestic urban context, emphasised by its historic and symbolic association with the Jerónimos Monastery and the River Tagus. The extraordinary value of this area of landscape has been given due recognition by its inclusion on UNESCO's list of World Heritage Sites.

This guide, published in partnership between IPPAR and Scala Publishers, is designed to provide the public with the necessary information to help them understand the architecture and history of the Torre de Belém, at the same time as revealing a little more of what, for many, is still surrounded in myth.

João Belo Rodeia
(President of IPPAR)

TORRE DE BELÉM

THE TAGUS

The Tagus has played a fundamental role in long- and short-distance trade since the Middle Ages. Its immense estuary with an inner bay, the Mar da Palha, served as a major shipping route with various crossing points between the two riverbanks; between, that is, the city of Lisbon itself and the manufacturing sites for the countless consumer goods required by the seafarers for their journeys. The great river which flowed in to the estuary was also easily navigable in its lower reaches.

These fledgling forms of industrial production grew significantly in the fifteenth century, at a time when Portuguese expansion in North Africa and along the west coast of Africa was accelerating. In the sixteenth century industrial production began to develop on the riverbank to the south, where biscuits and ceramic containers were produced, and also boats of light or medium draught, following an economic trend that dated back to Roman times. The north bank, with the great boatyards of the Ribeira das Naus – where the largest vessels in Europe were built – established a relationship of interdependence with the south bank. The navigability of the Tagus, although slowly diminishing due to the gradual silting up of the river (it was still possible to travel as far as Golegã in light-draught boats), made the veritable inland sea of the Mar da Palha – dubbed a 'miniature Mediterranean' – critically important.

The city tucked away on its north bank, a fair distance from the actual mouth of the Tagus, in a secluded and protected place, grew exponentially during the fifteenth and sixteenth centuries to become one of Europe's major cities – and undoubtedly its most important port in terms of long-distance navigation, after the discovery of the New World and the sea route to India. The many imports from distant exotic lands literally poured into Lisbon, which consequently became the principal centre for their trade. It could with reason be said that just about everything was to be found in Lisbon. China, spices, precious stones, ivory and furniture were all sold on the famous Rua Nova dos Mercadores, the street with the highest concentration of rich merchants in Europe at the time. With it grew an appetite for the new, and trends in fashion and consumption in general soon developed, creating a genuine 'luxury economy', based entirely on the potential for trade in sumptuous imported products and creating an ever-growing market. As royal chronicler Damião de Góis described it in his 1554 book *Urbis Olisiponis Descriptio* (*Description of the City of Lisbon*):

Below General view of the Torre de Belém. Present-day setting on the banks of the Tagus, showing its proximity to the riverbank with the water basin evoking its former 'island' status.

Opposite General view of the Torre de Belém.

'There are two cities which, in our times, we might justly refer to as ladies and (so to speak) queens of the Ocean since it is under their direction and control that shipping is today conducted throughout the Orient and Occident.

One of these cities is Lisbon, which claims dominion over that part of the Ocean which, from the mouth of the Tagus, takes in Africa and Asia in an immense maritime circuit. The other is Seville, from the river Guadalquivir to the West, which opened wide to navigation that part of the globe known today as the New World.'

As Lisbon acquired undeniable prestige on the oceanic and, specifically, the Atlantic front, lasting at least until the end of the sixteenth century, the river Tagus, on whose banks it stood, also developed its own reputation, as a result of the natural features of its harbour, the wealth of its traffic and the importance of its early industrial production sites – the boatyards, and the support products (rope, cooperage, arms, consumables). It came to be considered one of the world's major rivers, both in terms of symbolic geography and in terms of economic resources, a vital artery along which the riches of the world passed and where they were kept. Damião de Góis asserted in the same book: 'nowadays, this same river Tagus makes laws and regulations that are applied throughout all the coasts of the Ocean, in Africa and Asia. To these laws are subject, freely or by force, the kings and princes of those provinces, who render submission to the Portuguese, and many of them, in ever-growing numbers, live in obedience to the faith of

General view, showing the two main parts of the building's structure: the tower and, projecting into the Tagus, the bastion.

Christ. And this is done with the greatest veneration, not only in the dominions of the Indies, but also in the territories of the Chinese, and lands as far away as those of the Japanese, a people until recently unknown in Europe.' Indeed, the river Tagus and Lisbon were considered the real centres of the world economy, and also the point from which the evangelisation of the entire Globe set out, with obvious ideological and religious consequences.

But there was one problem that had to be resolved. The accumulation of wealth in Lisbon and the surrounding area, as well as the strategic importance of the river, made them attractive targets for raids by pirates, and the area's maritime frontiers were sometimes revealed as being rather too permeable, as they were poorly defended and watched over only by systems of watchtowers that were proving completely ineffective, especially following the development of artillery. The building of the Portuguese empire required the entrance of the Tagus to be properly protected from raids by pirates or corsairs. Additionally, there was a need to use military rhetoric as an effective and dissuasive defence system, making it sufficiently impressive and far-reaching to give a clear signal to the other European powers and their fleets that the river was protected and under sovereignty.

TECHNOLOGY IN THE TIME OF DOM JOÃO II

At the end of the fifteenth century, the first steps were taken to provide the river with this system of defence, at the royal initiative of Dom João II (1455-1495; r. 1481-1495). From a reading of the chronicles it can be deduced that priority was given to this undertaking by Dom João II. As the *Cronica de D. João II* (chap. CLXXXI) by Garcia de Resende (1545) tells us, the King turned his attention to establishing a genuine overall defence system, which would include the so-called 'bar' or entrance to the Tagus at its narrowest point, defined by Restelo on the north bank and Almada on the south bank (Paulina beach, next to Porto Brandão), and from there to the distant but strategic bay of the town of Cascais, facing the ocean:

'And so he then ordered the tower of Cascais to be built with its ditch, with enough and sufficiently large artillery to defend the port; and also another tower, and bastion at Caparica opposite Belém, in which there was much heavy artillery, and he ordered a strong fortress to be

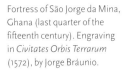

Fortress of São Jorge da Mina, Ghana (last quarter of the fifteenth century). Engraving in *Civitates Orbis Terrarum* (1572), by Jorge Bráunio.

built, where the beautiful Torre de Belém now stands, which King Dom Manoel, may God rest his soul, ordered to be built, so that the fortress on the one hand and the tower on the other should obstruct the entrance of the river. This fortress I drew at his command, and with him I disposed it according to his wishes, and he had already given the captaincy of it to Aluaro da Cunha, his master equerry, and a person in whom he placed great trust, and because the King then died, there was not time for it to be built, and his great ship, which was the biggest, strongest, and most well-armed ever seen, built to guard the river rather than to sail the seas. Which, placed at anchor in the middle of the river, alone defended it, as would the fortress and tower, because it was the biggest, strongest and most well-armed ship that was ever seen.'

The system then conceived was supposed to ensure the protection of the river entrance by artillery firepower, which represented a significant technological advance. At the end of the reign of Dom João II, in the 1480s and early 1490s, the *Torre da Caparica* or *Torre de São Sebastião*, later known as the 'Torre Velha' or Old Tower, was built on the steep slope of the south bank on the site of Paulina beach, at the point where the river is narrowest; and the *Torre de Cascais*, on the north point of the bay, today incorporated into the more recent construction of the fortress of Nossa Senhora da Luz. The tower on the north bank of the Tagus, which was to be sited opposite the Torre da Caparica, is the Torre de Belém, begun a great deal later, in the middle of the reign of Dom Manuel, almost certainly in 1514.

In all this, the exchange of ideas that the King and other noblemen with responsibilities in African trade may have had with fortification specialists and Italian military engineers would not have been surprising, in the context of the early Renaissance period and in some cases of 'Italianate' influence. The role played in Portuguese territorial expansion and in the development of maritime exploration by Dom João II began to be felt even when he was still a prince, when in 1474 his father, King Afonso V (1432-1481), granted him the trade and shipping of Guinea or, according to the documentation, entrusted him 'with the revenue and proceeds of the trade from Guinea, the fishing of its seas and rivers and everything discovered and yet to be discovered, and the rights that belonged to Infante Henrique, as well as the mission to explore these regions and seas'.

It is also worth pointing out that the reign of João II saw an active policy of civil and literary openness which had echoes in the field of arts and architecture, and this can be seen particularly in the designs selected for buildings constructed under royal patronage – such as the

Hospital Real das Caldas in Óbidos, or the Hospital Real Todos-os-Santos in Lisbon or the Fortress of São Jorge da Mina in Africa. The Hospital das Caldas is said to have been highly innovative, built in a T-shape, although with some irregularity, and topped by the construction of a small church, whose patron saint, Nossa Senhora do Pópulo, clearly expressed the Italianate affinities of those who commissioned. This church, probably designed by Mateus Fernandes, combined many of the elements that would later come to characterise the style known as 'Manueline'.

In the case of the Hospital Real in Lisbon, its design was entirely new, possibly based on examples seen in Italy – such as the Hospedale Maggiore in Milan – with its wards arranged around courtyards, and it was the first civil and public building designed on the plan of a cross. The wards, with hygiene conditions unusual for the time and systems for the circulation of patients, all pointed towards the chancel of the church, which could be seen by all the patients from their beds, thus creating a means for the cure of sickness to be related to the presence of faith through the accompaniment of the divine office. This magnificent building, sadly no longer in existence, can be described as an unrivalled architectural specimen. It was not completed until the reign of Dom Manuel, who added an overtly 'Manueline' façade to its church, with thick cable decorations and portentous heraldry, contrasting with the rationality and plainness of the rest of the building's façade, whose low arcades, overlooking the great Rossio square, used to shelter pilgrims and dispense first aid. From what we can tell from the evidence that has come

The system of fortifications at the entrance of the Tagus in the time of Dom João II: representation of the Torre de Cascais. Engraving in *Civitates Orbis Terrarum* (1572), by Jorge Bráunio.

down to us, it must have been one of the most striking buildings in the monumental topography of Lisbon until the end of the eighteenth century, with an ordered cross-shaped plan and a tall church tower standing out in the middle crowned by a pyramidal slate roof.

In its turn, the Fortress of São Jorge da Mina on the Gold Coast was to be the first great European fortress to be built overseas. This building, on a quadrangular plan, consisted of an exterior walled square with cuboid turrets at the corners protecting a large keep, which, in spite of everything, was still an important symbol of royal power. On top – as with the Igreja das Caldas – Dom João II ordered the building of swallowtail battlements, which would at the time have had universally understood 'Caesarist' or imperial connotations. It was indeed important, at that point in the final quarter of the fifteenth century, to devise and exhibit a strategy for

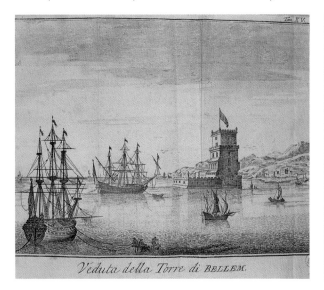

Veduta della Torre di BELLEM.

Vue de la Tour de BELLEM.

consolidating the undeniable advances of Portugal's maritime expansion, which culminated in the rounding the Cape of Good Hope by Bartolomeu Dias. The fortification stood mid-way along this route, in what is now Ghana. It was completed in the 1480s, and while still 'medieval' in some aspects of its design, it was monumental and absolutely decisive in the 'globalising' or planetary territorial demarcation that Dom João II aspired to. It was an authentic 'castle in Africa' the like of which did not exist – and never would exist – anywhere else. At that time, too, new towns were being built – such as Vila Nova de Milfontes and Vila das Caldas de Óbidos, as it was then known – and civil engineering projects were being undertaken, such as the Cano Aqueduct in Setúbal. It was a time of innovation and territorial intervention without any immediate precedent, although, as Rafael Moreira has pointed out, earlier initiatives of private patronage, such as those of Dom Afonso, Count of Ourém, do show similar early Renaissance inclinations in their technical and architectural preferences, as can be seen clearly in the Castelo de Ourém or the Castelo de Porto Mós.

The remodelling of the stronghold of Olivença also dates from the time of Dom João II. Here a large exterior ditch or moat was dug and the keep was made larger. It was enormous, indeed one of the most substantial of any built on continental territory, with a characteristic thick base to the wall, a profile that was later used in the Torre de Belém.

It is clear that architecture played an important role in the options of the State and its dominions at that time, particularly military architecture – and was absolutely essential in the macro-political context of Portugal's territorial expansion in Africa. To such an extent, as the researcher Pedro Cid has pointed out, that 'Suddenly, in fourteen years of a reign that changed

Above *Vue de la Tour de Belém*; French engraving from the seventeenth century.

Above left *Vedutta della Torre di Bellem*; Italian engraving from the seventeenth century.

Opposite *The Torre de Belém in the nineteenth century.* Oil on canvas, English school, nineteenth century, Museu da Cidade. You can still see the barracks built in the reign of the Philips on the terrace of the bastion and the crowning of the bastion with artillery battlements. Here the tower is still separated from the land.

15

the face of the Country, there was a real upsurge in the use of "paintings", "drawings", "sets of plans": words that began to appear frequently in the documentation of the period, along with allusions to constructions that are "ordered", "mediated" or "drawn".' If we consider that the use of drawings in the design of very large buildings was perhaps introduced at the end of the reign of Dom João I, and specifically with the construction of the Batalha Monastery (which might be called the 'explosion' of Gothic design), there is little doubt that the practice became widespread in the time of Dom João II due to the requirements of fortification overseas at great distances (hence the '*sets of plans*' and '*drawings*', which would have to be examined and appraised in the court for practical and commissioning purposes), and went on to become common practice in the reign of his successor Dom Manuel.

This means that it was in the time of Dom João II that the impetus developed for the transition from a rather 'organic' culture, conducted in an ad hoc way – which we might refer to as medieval – to a 'modern' culture of planning, not unfamiliar in fields of knowledge other than architecture, with the development of the geometric measurement of space, cartography, astronomy, mathematics and geography, with the gradual rationalisation of the politics of trade, and with the construction of a scientific *corpus* that infiltrated all the arts and all the sectors spawned by expansion.

The contracting of the illustrious Italian artist Andrea de Sansovino and his arrival in Portugal between 1492 and 1501 coincided with this exceptional period, as Rafael Moreira's masterful study shows. But it does not always seem to have been strictly the artistic aspect that most interested the King. In fact, the technological modernisation undertaken by Portugal in order to guarantee its territorial and maritime supremacy was a determining factor in the growth in cultural interchanges between Portugal and the Italian kingdoms. Exchanges of information on geographical matters with the famous Paolo Toscanelli, contacts with the engineer Jacopo Mariano Taccola (who was a student of Leonardo), the contracting of the expert Lourenço Florentim in 1469 to organise the operation of the mines of Adiça, or the invitation extended by Dom João II in 1492 (and renewed by Dom Manuel I in 1506) to metallurgist Paolo Savetti, are but a few instances which throw an entirely new light on a period in which intense investment in technology was going on side by side with the aesthetic approach anchored in a clearly 'Florentine' taste which explains the commissioning of Attavanti, in 1494, to produce illuminated books – such as the '*Comentários da Bíblia*' [Commentaries on the Bible] by Nicolau de Lira for the Jerónimos Monastery.

Andrea de Sansovino remained in Portugal for nine years and during that time, as much or perhaps more than occupying himself in the production of works of art, he became absorbed in the invention of useful devices. In addition to inventing a '*mechanical saw*' which '*he made in Portugal*' for the extraction of jasper (undoubtedly from the chasm of Arrábida), then highly sought-after for its reddish colour and symbolic value, it is thought that Andrea may have collaborated in the trial installations of low-angle firing artillery from the bulge of caravels or in planning the defence of the entrance to the Tagus. This is no more than speculation, since there would certainly have been other specialists in Portugal capable of developing this pioneering and experimental military work.

Resende says in this respect that '... Because the King... saw that to guard the strait [the entrance to the Tagus] from Moorish ships, and the coast from pirates, a great deal was being spent on fleets of large ships, that he ordered to be built for this purpose, as he was a talented man... in all arts, and he knew a great deal about artillery... here in Setúbal, with many experiments, he devised and ordered large cannons to be put into small caravels, and they drew so low that they touched the water... And just a few caravels... chased away many large ships... and being very light and small, the large ships could not harm them with their shots, the caravels of Portugal were greatly feared on the sea for a long time, so that no ships, no matter how large, dared wait for them, until it was known how they were able to fire such shots, and they are used today as in other places'.

Clearly the defence of the entrance of the Tagus was of great concern to Dom João II, to the point of promoting such experiments, carried out by German seamen and artillery-men, in which large-calibre bombards were installed aboard caravels, in port flaps in the hull very close to the waterline. The shots were therefore fired at a very low angle or even, using a surprisingly complex process, consisted of rebound shots with the cannonballs bouncing on the water. What was at issue here was the effectiveness of firing against ships, given that the simple high-flying discharge with the usual artillery trajectory either missed the ship that was its target, or hit its mark but only caused minor damage because it fell onto it rather than breaching it from the side. The sweeping or low-angle shot and even more the rebound shot (if they managed to carry it off, which required great skill) meant that cannonballs penetrated the ship's hull close to the waterline, as the calculations of Lieutenant Colonel Varela Rubim demonstrated, causing much more serious damage. Given that this type of firing over water from a ship would be extremely difficult to execute, it is highly probable that Dom João II had in mind its use not only on caravels or 'naus' (and from these, only as low-angle fire), but also or more especially from fixed firing platforms on the coast. This experience would certainly have been at the basis of the design of the Torre de Belém.

THE 'FORTRESS' OF BELÉM

Returning to Garcia de Resende, we find a particular reference to his involvement in devising the programme of defence of the entrance of the Tagus, specifically alluding to the Torre de Belém: 'Which fortress I drew at his command, and disposed with him according to his wishes…'. This has led to some confusion and for a long time the design of the Torre de Belém was attributed erroneously to Garcia de Resende himself.

It was not until 1922 that art historian Reinaldo dos Santos cleared up the doubt, correctly attributing the design to the architect of the Manueline period Francisco de Arruda. Still more curious is the fact that Garcia de Resende was indeed a good 'debuxador' or draughtsman, appreciated by Dom João II in this art, and he could well have produced a sketch, drawing or 'mostra' (set of plans) of a fortress for the Restelo site. As various researchers have pointed out, however, close examination of the words actually used by Resende in this passage is required for us to draw the correct conclusion from it; Resende in fact refers to a 'fortaleza' or fortress and not a 'torre' or tower. In the words of Pedro Cid, Resende mentions an 'architectural object whose "project" would have been drawn up between the monarch and Resende himself (his clerk at the time), with the respective "debuxo" or drawing being made by the latter, under the direct supervision of the King'. Reiterating the analysis, we quote Pedro Cid when he concluded – rightly, in our opinion – 'that it was Dom João II himself, who, with the help of Garcia de Resende, planned the initial fortress, the decisive role in defining its architecture and design, in all probability, having fallen to the King (a conclusion that the sixteenth-century text undoubtedly suggests and which, being perhaps surprising, reflects a Perfect Prince acting, on certain constructions, as a lot more than mere commissioner of the work)'. And he adds: 'What would this fortress have been like? If we consider other military constructions from the reign of Dom João II – such as the castles of São Jorge da Mina and of Tangiers, the 'great tower' and 'ditch' of Olivença, the primitive bastions of Elvas and Montalegre, the Torre de Cascais (all of them pioneering examples) - we believe that it would have followed a fairly sophisticated organisational plan.'

This is a plausible hypothesis, in spite of the fact that the design of the fortress and tower that was eventually built is undeniably that of Francisco de Arruda. It is probable, in our view, that some of the suggestions that had been outlined by Dom João II and Resende, may have been at the basis of the association of the style of the tower with the style – original in Dom Manuel's time – of the bastion. After all, the experience of construction of the so-called Torre da Caparica (combining a parallelepiped tower with a 'fortress' for low-angle fire), built in the time of Dom João II, will undoubtedly have influenced Arruda's design. It was part of the technical heritage that he had at his disposal.

For the siting of what would become the Torre Velha de São Sebastião and of the future fortress on the Restelo side, Dom João II would certainly have ordered surveys to be carried out, as was customary at the time. These surveys would have been detailed. They would have taken into consideration the topography of the riverbanks and what was already there; for

Hexagonal bastion; general view of the east face, lined in lias limestone. Note the striking scenic effect of the battlements, with shields with the Cross of Christ in relief, copied from the parapet of the tower.

Right Tower and bastion in their present position on the coast.

example, Paulina beach as a landing place, but also Porto Brandão and its small bay, where the workers of the boatyards of the Tagus lived on the south bank, and the settlement of Restelo on the north bank. They would certainly have taken into account the fact that a well-known and very well-used river-crossing passage had existed between Restelo and Porto Brandão since the Middle Ages, as well as the profile of the riverbanks and the most suitable places for the construction of the fortresses, both in terms of strategic position and in terms of geological conditions. The place chosen for building the two principal defences of the river entrance would have to be located at the precise point at which the Tagus was narrowest: in the south, Paulina beach and the steep hill behind it for the construction of the Torre Velha, completed in the time of Dom João II; in the north, what was probably a rocky basalt outcrop, situated well into the river, for the 'fortaleza' or fortress that Resende drew, but which was not built until Dom Manuel's reign. In actual fact, the aim was to apply to maritime defence a basic principle of artillery defence: the use of crossfire between two points in order to cover the whole area of the river entrance.

This was of course the place where the great sentinel and defensive '*nau*' which had patrolled the river since the time of Dom João II usually anchored. Indeed, the purpose of building these two defensive structures was to replace this extraordinary and monumental man-of-war. Recalling the words of Resende, which were no exaggeration, this was the 'great ship, which was the biggest, strongest, and most well-armed that was ever seen', and which according to him was 'built to guard the river rather than to sail the seas. Which, placed at anchor in the middle of the river, alone defended it, as would the fortress and tower.' This huge man-of-war would have been of the largest 'class' of all those that were built at the Ribeira boatyards – and would have been the biggest at the time in the whole of Europe. As Pedro Cid pointed out, the name (or patron saint) of the ship – São Cristóvão or Saint Christopher, the giant saint who carried Christ across a river on his back – was very apposite for a ship of this vast size, which displaced nearly 1000 tonnes. Its immense outward curve housed an impressive quantity of artillery (more than thirty large cannons and nearly two hundred small cannons). 'Placed at anchor in the middle of the river', it constituted a genuine firing platform in the middle of the water. The Torre de Belém was to retain in evocative terms, in its morphology and decoration, the memory of this 'great ship'.

THE NEW DEFENCE OF THE ENTRANCE OF THE TAGUS

Once the studies had been carried out, a proposal was made for a strategic arrangement of firing fortresses positioned, finally, at three key points: Cascais, at the point where the sea meets the mouth of the estuary; Porto Brandão, on the south bank of the Tagus, opposite Restelo; and on Restelo itself – where the Torre de Belém now stands. Clear and significant testimony to this defence system remains.

In Cascais, in the Fortaleza de Nossa Senhora da Luz, structures still remain from Dom João's time, today assimilated into the star-shaped bastion built in the time of the Philip kings, which in turn has been assimilated by the walls of the great citadel of Cascais. Part of the architectural structure built by Dom João II was revealed during archaeological work carried out by Margarida Magalhães Ramalho. Of the contents of the bastion, the tower that crowned this defence system remains almost intact. According to the depictions that have come down to us (specifically, an engraving of Cascais in the book by Jorge Bráunio, *Civitate Orbis Terrarum*, 1572), this was a mixed defence system. It had a large open-air firing platform, situated high above the pleasant inlet. Further back, this platform had a 'medieval'-type tower. In addition to this, there were simpler casemated constructions, to house the garrison and the magazine. Dom João II's aim was to promote the building of an active system, on a small promontory sticking out into the sea, in contrast with the passive system – still represented today by the ruins of the Guia tower, which was no more than a watchtower – to prevent the bay being used, as it is documented to have been used on various occasions, as shelter for the vessels of pirates and corsairs. It might reasonably be considered an early prototype of the Torre de Belém, although lacking its unity or homogeneity and the more effective integration of its various components (the platform, an early kind of bastion; the tower, and the support buildings). And like the Torre de Belém – as we shall see later – it served to protect the beach and the inlet but not, in this case, to provide crossfire with another defence system, since this would only have been possible given the presence of a ship to create a narrower access corridor.

On the Porto Brandão side, or more specifically on Paulina beach, stood the Torre Velha de São Sebastião da Caparica, built – like the one just described – in the time of Dom João II. This fortress, studied in depth by Pedro Cid, is a fascinating firearm defence system designed according to the most advanced principles of military architecture of its time. It owes nothing to Italian designs, but instead represents a genuine embodiment of what had previously been merely drawn or imagined.

It has a broad quadrangular tower, standing on a defensive wall which allows communication with the lowest storey at river level, a wall which makes partial use of the steep natural slope. The various components of this interesting construction can be distinguished: at the lowest level, next to the river (where there is now a quay), was the bastion itself, on a trapezoidal plan, with apertures to allow the famous low-angle fire and a large terrace for manoeuvring. Above it rose the wall, '*acasamatada*' or casemated, in the words of Pedro Cid, which linked the bastion itself with the tower. Its interior was pierced by a staircase, leading vertically from the terrace or lower platform to the upper terrace and the entrance to the tower itself. The tower, which still stands on the steep slope, was a parallelepiped, with an open-air upper terrace with embellished corners, and the remaining construction built of stone covered in plaster, without any ornament worthy of note, as though sobriety were an imperative there. In the interior was an apartment with a fireplace, possibly divided into two floors, for the governor of the Torre Velha. Few doubts remain that this was a pioneering structure, possibly taking its inspiration from the treatises of Francesco de Giorgio Martini. Strictly speaking, the Torre Velha – when it was in operation – possessed everything in warlike apparatus that the Torre de Belém would later lack, for the latter is far more decorative than martial, as we shall see.

The fortress planned for the north bank, already outlined or sketched, was to make way, nearly fifteen years later, for the Torre de Belém. The Torre de Belém, while built on different stylistic principles (although still in the category which historians of military architecture call 'transitional style'), would have to comply, in a more rhetorical and imposing way, with the precepts already used in the Torre Velha, only now in a more 'concentrated' area, since it was to stand on an existing outcrop (or stony breakwater) in the river. Indeed it is this very density and the closeness of its various elements that make the tower so distinctively original and impressive.

With regards to the construction of the Torre de Belém, it is important to note a letter written to Dom Manuel around December 1513 (possibly before construction began) by Lourenço Fernandes: '... and I say, Senhor, that some friends of master builder Boytac say now that the King sent for him, to come and build a tower on old Restelo, which certainly, Senhor, is very necessary; and to anyone who thinks the contrary, if he were to suffer the attacks that I have experienced, since I have been here, he would see the need for it, which I shall not describe for the sake of brevity and because it would in a way be in my praise, Senhor, in addition to being here as fort governor, for believe that as such I have found myself many times under attack, which has been resisted by me, with the help of my men, in the service of your highness, which if there were a tower would not happen...'. This strange letter, brought to light by researcher Mário Sampayo Ribeiro, points up two relevant facts: the urgent need for a tower to be built at Belém for military reasons, which were still pressing in 1513; and the idea, put forward by Lourenço Fernandes, that it was Diogo Boytac who was intended as master builder of the building to be constructed. Further, the letter indicates that the tower had been planned for a long time, as this is what Lourenço Fernandes gives us to understand when he complains of the lack of conditions to guarantee the security of that route. Could this difficulty have been revealed by some attempted aggression against what was then the major construction site of the Jerónimos Monastery? If this is the case, and there is nothing to contradict it, the theory that the Torre de Belém would have served as protection for the construction site might in a way be turned on its head. In other words, if a tower or fortress had been planned for that site since the time of Dom João II, the building of the Mosteiro de Santa Maria de Belém might have been inspired not only by the existence of a hermitage founded by Infante Dom Henrique for the protection of seafarers – Nossa Senhora do Restelo – which would undoubtedly be the principal reason for the building of a great monastic house, but also by the knowledge that this

Hexagonal bastion; general view of the west face. The cannon apertures are positioned low down to enable low-angle firing.

site would sooner or later be fortified or strategically defended from coastal incursions, in spite of its evident vulnerability. This point was later emphasised by Damião de Góis when he stated in his *Descriptio*: 'In the front part of the church [Jerónimos], stands a tower four storeys high, built of ashlar stone, which Dom Manuel ordered to be built on rocks out in the sea, in such a way that, surrounded by water on all sides, it would remain secure against any violence and sudden attack by enemies'.

With regards to the appearance of master builder Diogo Boytac, in the argument of the embattled 'fort governor', as the proposed builder of the Tower that was to be constructed, there seems nothing to contradict this either. It is known that Boytac enjoyed immense prestige in the court of Dom Manuel. Diogo Boytac was already active in the reign of Dom João II, having directed the building work of the innovative Convent of Jesus in Setúbal with its hall-church since around 1490. He played a prominent role on the construction site of Batalha – which became his adopted home – by virtue of his two ties of relationship with the heirs of veteran master builder Mateus Fernandes (who was his son-in-law) and from the responsibilities he discharged in the construction of the great monastic house. He appears to have worked on another project initiated by Dom João II, the Hospital Real de Todos-os-Santos in Lisbon (finishing what was probably begun by Mateus Fernandes), and certainly drew the plans for the main entrance, at the same time as he began his work on Santa Maria de Belém (i.e. around 1501). In 1507 he began the reconstruction of the Santa Cruz Monastery in Coimbra, and signed a second contract in 1513. At the same time he was involved in the Pena Convent in Sintra and in the project for the Santa Ana Convent in Leiria, no longer in existence. His work in the field of military architecture was well-known; he was in Arzila in 1510, and travelled to North Africa again in 1514 and 1515, where he supervised the building of fortresses and participated in the ill-fated expedition to Mármora. It is possible that Boytac's responsibility for the unfortunate outcome of that expedition may have contributed to the loss of the King's confidence and to his dismissal from the post of master builder on the Santa Maria de Belém monastery, where his presence is documented until 1516, in charge of a project involving over a hundred journeymen.

His role at Belém was a major one, since it is to him that we owe the plan of the monastery, transposing the design of the Setúbal construction onto a much more ambitious scale. He was a well-known figure in courtly circles and his status was so high that a sentence he addressed to the king, against the Baron of Alvito, is recorded for posterity: 'Your Highness can make as many barons as he wishes but he cannot make a master Butaca'. His skill must have been highly regarded, at least until the events in Mauritania in 1515, to the extent that Dom António de Noronha openly interrupted the Spanish soldier Diego de Medina – 'hold his tongue, for where mestre Butaqua was, no one was to talk', an incident related in a letter in which the Spaniard complains to the monarch of this affront to his authority. As we know, however, completion of the work on Santa Maria de Belém did not fall to Boytac. In April 1516 João de Castilho came on the scene and remained there side by side with Boytac until taking over full administration of the construction site on 2 January 1517. Diogo Boytac then disappears from the documentation and there were probably two reasons for this: his fall from grace with the King, already mentioned, due to the military disaster of Mármora, for which his proverbial stubbornness and possibly his outdated approach in the face of advances in military technology, and military architecture in particular, were considered responsible; and the difficulties in sorting out the vaulting of the church.

THE CONSTRUCTION OF THE TORRE DE BELÉM

Dom Manuel's choice of who to commission to carry out this project fell, finally, on master builder Francisco de Arruda, an expert in defensive structures, whose long career on the continent and overseas gave evidence of great experience, as we shall see. The attribution of the design to Francisco de Arruda, older brother of another notable Manueline architect, Diogo de Arruda, with whom he collaborated closely, has been made on the basis of documents that refer to him, in 1516, as 'master builder of the Bastion of Restelo', mentioning him as the recipient of a large quantity of 'blocks of stone', in other words, ashlar masonry already prepared in the quarry for the construction. The work was already under way in 1515, the earliest documented date referring to the building.

At that time the major construction project of the Jerónimos Monastery was already in full swing and was shortly to receive a new impetus and a new arrangement, as we have already seen.

The Tower thus conceived would have been intended not just to defend the narrowest passage of the Tagus, but also now to protect the great monastery and the riches that were housed in the church. According to Damião de Góis in his *Chronica do Felicíssimo Rei Dom Emmanuel*, 1566/1567 [Chronicle of the Most Fortunate King Manuel], continuing what he wrote in his *Descriptio*, but giving it greater emphasis: 'In front of this building the King ordered to be built the tower of St. Vincent, which is called tower of Belém, in the water, to guard this Monastery and the port of Lisbon, a building which although not large in itself, is nevertheless magnificent in its structure. The said tower is watched over by night and by day such that no sail may pass by without being seen and yielding to the volleys of gunfire that are fired from it.'

This goes a long way towards explaining the morphology of the Tower and its ornamental opulence, which both accorded with current taste and was suited to its location on the bank of the river, already being turned into a place of monumental grandeur. The magnificent portal of the south façade of the Jerónimos Monastery, completed around 1517, served as a genuine 'triumphal arch' or 'gateway through which the triumphs of the conquest of the Orient should enter into this kingdom', in the words of João de Barros, forming a magnificent architectural complex to impress anyone entering the Tagus, and of which the Torre de Belém was to be an integral part.

The Torre de Belém is built in the late-Gothic Portuguese style known as 'Manueline' and, with its hyperrealism, its heavy ornamentation and its unredeemed attachment to heraldry (a reflection of a courtly mentality still linked to the mythography of medieval chivalry) clearly shows the principal elements of this style which obstinately resisted the influences of Renaissance classicism.

STRUCTURE

The Torre de Belém was built on an existing basalt outcrop some distance from the north bank of the Tagus, which is presumed to have been levelled and built up with the addition of stones deposited to create a foundation.

The structure of the building can be summed up fairly simply. It is composed of a hexagonal bastion topped by a tower at the back, medieval in form. It thus combines a modern military defence system – strictly speaking, the first of its type to be built in Portugal – with a medieval military defensive system, the traditional 'tower', summing up the very essence of Manueline architecture. This was no compromise solution, it was rather a transitional solution between the new warfare of firearms, involving heavy artillery cannon and low-angle firing, and the old methods of warfare, involving the hurling of projectiles. In other words the long low bastion, a pioneering construction, almost flat and at water-level, was introduced, or we might say proclaimed, by the traditional image of seigniorial power embodied in the tower. This was the plan.

In terms of the principles of the design, it can be seen that the calculation was based on the proportion 1:1. The plan of the tower is a quarter of the size of the plan of the set-back section of the bastion, with a square base. It was displaced towards the axis of the composition, straddling the bastion.

How was this design arrived at? No doubt through an accumulation of recent experience on the part of Portuguese military architects, but it was also the fruit of a self-taught study of pioneering design sources. Opposite Belém there already stood the unusual structure of the Torre Velha, which however lacked any rhetorical effects, or rather, any decorative effects; and not far from there stood the Fortress of Cascais, combining, although in a different way, a firing platform with a vertical structure. The researcher João Néu drew attention to a passage in one of the letters sent to Dom Manuel by Afonso de Albuquerque, in which he mentions a fortification built by master builder Tomás Fernandes (another significant name in the Portuguese art of fortification) at Benastarim in India, describing it as a 'tower (...) four storeys in height, which can be seen from the walls of Goa. On the first floor stood a tower next to it on the bank of the river, built of timber on pillars and roofed with a terrace: it faces dry land, towards which it can

Opposite Fortress model, according to Francesco di Giorgio Martini. Once again we can see the combination of a tower-shaped structure with a platform for firing bombards, culminating at the lowest point in a small triangular bastion.

Below *Fortress of Cagli.* Drawing by Francesco di Giorgio Martini. You can see the combination of a large tower with structures which are already similar in form to bastions extending outwards below.

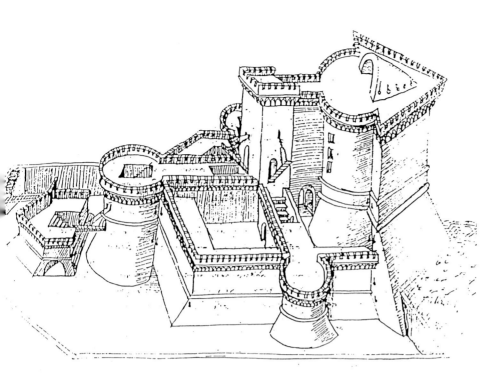

hurl heavy artillery; and another tower rose three floors above it'. He adds yet another example of a tower integrated into the defensive system of Goa, mentioned by Gaspar Correia, which would have been built around 1510, on the river Mandovi: 'and he built two square towers, one for the city in the area of Mandovim, the other on the gate of the quay (...) and from the tower of Mandovim he built a wall with an outer defensive wall for an eight-sided bastion, which he built on the river, with its cannons between wind and water'. It seems clear that a practical culture circulated among Portuguese fortification builders, who had already incorporated in practical terms the combination of firing platforms with a tower, whether as temporary constructions in which wood was used as an essential component, or more permanent ones, as in the example of the Torre do Mandovi, which must have been similar in many respects to Belém, notably in the design of the polygonal outer wall.

In this context, the work of the Italian Francesco di Giorgio Martini (1439-1501), a military engineer and inventor and also an associate of Savetti and friend of Leonardo da Vinci, no less, assumes particular importance, as was rightly determined by the research of Rafael Moreira and more recently that of Pedro Cid. Martini seems to have had a significant indirect influence on the field of military architecture in Portugal. The pioneering technical and military approach of the Torre de Belém (and of the older Torre Velha) can only be explained by the deduction that Francisco de Arruda – and his older brother, Diogo – were certainly familiar with Martini's proposals for 'complex fortresses' drawn and explained in his principal work, *Architettura civile e militare* (1478-1492), various versions of which exist, among them, for our particular area of interest, the *Códice Magliabechiano*, dated 1480-1492 (specifically pages 68, 69 and 79 r.).

This Codex depicts extremely complex structures with multiple floors which, like the Torre de Belém, combine the new bastion with tower-shaped structures with merlons and balconies from which projectiles could be hurled downwards, and in some cases very similar to the probable original configuration of the Torre Velha, which stood opposite and which was probably designed by Diogo de Arruda.

Among Francesco di Giorgio Martini's designs with the most inventive points of contact with the Torre de Belém, is the Fortress of Cagli. In this example, Francesco combines a large tower with two outer defensive walls arranged like bastions with firing platforms. The tower is crowned with merlons. The double bastioned structure is also crowned with merlons and the 'outer' section has a triangular-shaped plan, advancing over a scarp. The 'inner' section of the bastion, situated at a slightly higher level, has a parapet or *chemin de ronde* and two circular firing platforms. The predominance of cylindrical structures in Frencesco's drawings, although they do not appear in the design of the Torre de Belém, still find an echo in the finish of each of the corners of the building, consisting invariably of cylindrical watchtowers. An even more intricate version of this design is one of Martini's fortress designs, in which there are several firing terraces and towers, integrated with the walls, with parapets which then splay out into platforms and with systems of communication pierced through the walls, as in the arrangement of the casemate of the bastion and its terrace. We should also point out, with regard to these relationships, the advanced bastion, triangular in shape (which might have inspired the polygonal shape of the bastion of the Torre de Belém), situated at the foremost point of all these fortifications.

Entrance gateway to the bastion; Plateresque decoration of chimeras and plant motifs.

THE BASTION

The bastion is the most unusual part of the whole structure. It consists of a hexagonal platform, with the base of the hexagon facing dry land. It is a low and sturdy construction, which might be called 'hydrodynamic', with its wall thicker at the base, and which stands in turn on the basalt outcrop – or foundation stones – on the bed of the river Tagus. Like the rest of the tower, the bastion was built entirely of white lias limestone with an infill of large bricks and stones in the vaults. Its protuberant thick base derives from fifteenth-century fortification techniques, with the base of the wall strengthened to offer a greater surface of embedment, both to prevent undermining and to deflect projectiles.

Access to the interior of the bastion – or more properly the casemate – is via a small drawbridge hidden by the projection that separates the bastion proper from the tower by means of a small section of wall, forming a discreet barbican. The entrance is a semi-circular arch with Plateresque decorative mouldings, among them some conspicuously fantastical motifs, notably the monstrous face of a hybrid creature located near the base. It would not be surprising if this doorway had been carved at the construction site of the Jerónimos monastery by an artist working on Castilho's project, and then brought here for installation.

Along this structure runs a functional U-shaped gallery used as the cannon battery. It is roofed by a robust rib vault with the cells supported by simple crossed ribs, devoid of any decoration. Note that the vaults spring practically from floor level. Rectangular hatchways open at intervals in the cells of the vault to let in light. The cannon apertures, 17 in number, are at the end of very deep segmented arch embrasures. They give a clear view of the river, being very close to water level, thus making low-angle fire possible. Behind them there is now a small cloister, its present form dating from the nineteenth-century restoration, with small arches and capitals forming a central space which was once used as a vent for releasing the smoke of the cannons. In the cellar below is the magazine, which was used at one time as a political prison – one of the most feared in the kingdom due to the damp.

Above this structure, up a simple flight of steps, is the terrace. Here further artillery complemented the cannons housed in the casemate. From this terrace, transformed several times (notably when a barracks was built here in 1589, as depicted in views from the early nineteenth century) there is an exceptional view over the river Tagus and towards the south bank. The top of the original vent for releasing the smoke – the small cloister – was decorated in the nineteenth century with a balcony laced with motifs of the Order of Christ, neo-Manueline pinnacles and gargoyles (one of which is a monkey playing a violin), to which an image of the Virgin was added, standing in a baldachin (an unlikely and somewhat anachronistic image on a building of a military nature).

Although the extent of the nineteenth-century restorations of the bastion remains as yet uncertain, the whole terrace is crowned with battlements, built like the pavises or shields of a ship and attached to the outside of the wall – a motif which is also found on one of the upper floors of the tower, which was not subjected to alterations during the restoration. It is indeed true that this 'seafaring' allusion, as Rafael Moreira points out, is one of the distinctive features

Left Interior of the bastion; casemate. At the top, opened in the panels of the vault, you can see the trap doors to let light in and smoke out.

Opposite Interior of the bastion; casemate, roofed with rib vaulting and plastered brickwork. You can see the thickness of the arches and the depth of the cannon embrasures. This was the operational or manoeuvre area for the men firing the cannons.

Opposite below Detail of the cannon embrasure with its deep curved section cut into the thickness of the perimeter walls.

of the Torre de Belém and may have served as a reminder of the 'great ship' formerly at anchor in the middle of the river.

Another architectural motif of great originality is the watchtowers on the corners of both bastion and tower. These are cylindrical constructions with look-out openings, roofed by a parachute dome capped by five balls (or 'cannonballs'). Some see in them allusions to the Arabic architecture of the Maghreb, or even inspirations from Indian architectural features. Such interpretations do not seem sustainable today, and caution should be exercised with regard to the possibility of their being a copy or reinvention of Mudéjar designs. What is certain is that the design of the small 'cylindrical house' with parachute dome had already appeared in the middle of the fourteenth century in the sculptural ornamentation of the Tomb of Dom Pedro in the Monastery of Alcobaça, and may have been more common than is supposed. The hypothesis should not be excluded, however, that the parachute dome might have a heraldic symbolism that is hard for us to understand today, in harmony with the rest of the ornamentation of the building.

The watchtowers are complemented in decorative terms by sturdy ropes or cables wrapped around them next to the conical console on which they are supported, marking the base of the dome. A rhinoceros (its nose, neck and front legs) is depicted on one of the consoles, undoubtedly a record of the magnificent animal – a white rhinoceros or 'ganda', the Indian name by

Left Staircase leading down to the underground floor, which was used as a magazine and store-room and later (in the eighteenth to nineteenth centuries) as a prison.

Below Detail of the entrance gateway; chimera.

which it was then known – which was an extraordinary gift from overseas to Dom Manuel from the sultan of Cambaia. Indeed, a fight was even organised between the rhinoceros and an elephant, in a specially built enclosure in Lisbon to be held in the presence of the king; but the elephant, not unwisely, fled in terror when it realised what its opponent was to be. The monarch presented the rhinoceros to Pope Leo X, on the occasion of the famous Portuguese mission to Rome, headed by Tristão da Cunha in 1514, but the animal later died at sea and was subsequently recovered and stuffed. It was this same rhinoceros that Dürer depicted in his no less famous engraving dated 1515. This is not the only sculpture of this animal, which reappears as one of the sixteenth-century gargoyles on the first floor of the Cloister of Silence in the monastery of Alcobaça, made a short time after this one. In any case, the representation of the rhinoceros on the console of the Torre de Belém is a useful indication of the tower's date, since it is unlikely that interest in the episode – and in the animal – would have continued much beyond the context of recent memory.

With regard to the effectiveness of firing from the bastion, the apertures of the embrasures in its lower part show that, in spite of being relatively narrow, they did give the cannons they housed a fair amount of room for manoeuvre, since these were not particularly heavy and allowed the angle of fire to be altered. But it seems certain that the function of the Torre de

Left Watchtower. You can see the coping with cannonballs (spheres), in turn surmounted by a ball, apple or grenade, possibly a symbolic reference to the North African conquests.

Below Profile of watchtower base, showing on the console the carving of the head of a rhinoceros given by Dom Manuel to Pope Leo X. This is the first depiction in stone of this exotic animal ever made anywhere in Europe.

Opposite above Platform or upper terrace of the bastion, where it overlooks the Tagus.

Opposite Interior staircase leading from the casemate to the terrace of the bastion.

Belém was not limited to crossfire with the Torre Velha situated opposite. Although lined up with this and with the São Jerónimo chapel, high on the wall of the Jeronymite monastery and a known observation point of the river, the Torre de Belém is set at an angle of 22°, which is evidence of the precise strategic thinking that lay behind the construction and of its functional purpose. João Néu studied the range of fire of each of the cannon apertures or gun ports, concluding that only three – specifically those open to the south – have firing directions straight across the river, with an interval of almost 45°. In other words, only these cannon apertures were suitable for crossing fire with the Torre Velha, situated almost 1670m away. The other apertures (with one exception) open on the west and east faces of the bastion, with straight lines of fire which are apparently redundant due to their concentration. There are eight such apertures in all, four on either side of the bastion. Taking a plan view, it can be seen that the shots that could be aimed from them were designed to protect the coast, preventing disembarkation on the beaches behind and on either side of the tower. This was one of the primary functions of the Torre de Belém. It is worth remembering that in the sixteenth century the Tower was around 200 to 250m off the coast, no small distance. The silting up of the river, and especially the silting up of the actual channel that ran between the tower and the riverbank, gathered pace during the seventeenth and eighteenth centuries, possibly due to the construction of the fortress itself, which acts as a ram leading to the accumulation of sediments on the coast and to the creation of beaches. In the nineteenth century, the Torre de Belém was already more or less joined to the land.

THE TOWER

From the bastion you get a sense of the imposing main façade of the tower. The treatment of the façade is extremely careful and delicate, contrasting dramatically with the austere atmosphere of the interior of the battery.

It is divided into four storeys. The first storey is completely plain, except for a single access door cut into it. The second is occupied by a full-length projecting balcony, with seven semicircular arches, standing on modillions. The third storey is decorated with a gigantic armillary sphere at either end, with the coat-of-arms of Portugal between two windows. The fourth storey is completely plain and set slightly back, with a parapet or *chemin de ronde* at its base, decorated with shield-shaped merlons with the crucifix carved on them. The top of the tower has watchtowers at the corners, of a similar design to those on the bastion but smaller in dimension, with pyramid-capped battlements running between them.

The sides and back of the tower are designed in a more discreet way, but nevertheless with devices that form an original combination of palatial architecture with traditional fortified military architecture. The presence should be noted of paired windows (at third floor level) and of small balconies with modillions, with paired Manueline bays and stone roofs, which are designed to look like a slate or tiled roof.

The faces of the tower also feature a carved rope, which runs around them horizontally and level with the terrace. On the north face this rope has a large central knot. On this face, above the watchtowers, is a niche on either side with a baldachin containing the images of Saint Vincent, patron saint of Lisbon, and the Archangel Michael, guardian angel of the kingdom.

Below left General view of the main façade of the tower, facing the Tagus. Note the proportion of the heraldic motifs, consisting of a royal shield and two armillary spheres, Dom Manuel's badge of office. This heraldic combination must have been similar to the one on the main façade of the other tower that marked the entrance to the city of Lisbon – on the Royal Palace, over the Tagus.

Below right Tower; general view of the west side.

Opposite View of the gallery or loggia from the inside. The scenic power of the feature is very clear here, notably in the decorative subtlety and a certain elegant fragility, appropriate to a palace.

Left Paired veranda, on machicolations; the military allusion is there, but softened by the elegant design of the projecting structures, with filigree balustrade (restored in the nineteenth century).

Opposite Main façade of the Tower. You can see the arrangement of its storeys and the way they are marked with purely architectural motifs – cornices and windows that reflect an architecture of representation and prestige.

Opposite below Detail of the double veranda. Note the imitation in stone of tiles of the roof.

This tower, in its military form and with its quadrangular section and large dimensions, undoubtedly took its inspiration from the most prestigious keeps that existed at the time. One such is the monumental tower that still stood on the bridge linked to the Ducal Palace of Barcelos, which was commissioned by Dom Afonso, eighth Count of Barcelos and powerful first Duke of Bragança, and was enormous in proportion and a parallelepiped in shape, with an upper floor surrounded by a continuous balcony on modillions. Other important towers to bear in mind are the keep of the castle at Estremoz, remodelled in the time of Dom João I, and especially the monumental keep at Beja (given that Dom Manuel was Duke of Beja before becoming king, and this would almost certainly have been a model considered in the conception of the tower). This magnificent building in the Alentejo, one of the most powerful pieces of medieval Portuguese military architecture, was certainly a model worthy of imitation or emulation. It is said that the Torre de Belém has several features reminiscent of the Torre de Beja, namely the faceting created by the stairwell, visible from the outside; the merlons capped with pyramids (on the coping); and, above all, the complex group of balconies and narrow galleries, which correspond in Beja (and in Estremoz) with the balconies on machicolations. There is a hypothesis that the projecting loggia, as well as the continuous balconies on the side faces of the tower, are the result of building in stone features that were traditionally constructed out of wood for festivals and events – in short, building in stone what had formerly been ephemeral architecture representing royal power, a frequent sight in Lisbon during the reign of Dom Manuel – but this has yet to be verified for want of more definite confirmation.

The more specifically military rather than palatial aspects of the tower's design – machicolations, *chemin de ronde* (parapet) with pavises, the upper terrace of the tower – these have been developed or moderated (or treated decoratively) to give a rhetorical representation of power and enhanced by an abundance of royal symbols, which take on truly striking proportions: the royal shields; the armillary spheres.

In addition to these symbols, cannonballs are represented on the watchtowers and in the interior 'flames' are used symbolically as eloquent ornamentation referring to the bastion's

artillery function. The galleries, the Manueline windows with Mudéjar features in their detailed ornamentation – such as the turban-shaped capitals – and the filigree balustrades which open on the four faces, give the Torre de Belém Levantine and Venetian connotations which, although denied by some authors, we consider one of the sources of inspiration of the architecture of the Arruda brothers, although reworked in accordance with the specific programme. It is also probable that points of contact exist with the palace architecture of Juan Guas, such as the Palacio del Duque del Infantado in Guadalajara, which is to say that the stylistic influence of Mudéjar architecture can be felt in terms of composition as well as in terms of specific features such as the capitals. Nothing could be more natural, in our view. Indeed, one of the most prestigious examples of Manueline palace architecture at the time was the National Palace at Sintra, which was profoundly influenced by the Mudéjar movement, notably in the use of verandas and windows with paired arches and galleries, in the parts added by Dom Manuel. Accepting this 'ostentatious' dimension for the tower (of the Torre de Belém), is to admit the influence of this aesthetic movement, particularly in an architectural piece that was linked to the Portuguese ambitions of expansion, principally in North Africa (the possible Moroccan inspiration of the parachute domes as being the *kottubia* of Marrakech, in spite of the already mentioned 'national' antecedents of micro-architecture, is not to be completely excluded). This North African characteristic, curiously fused with purely European elements and mingled with military features, was to become one of the trademarks of the architecture of the Arruda brothers.

Note too, certain persistent features of the design which seem to relate to formal tendencies almost exclusive to the architecture of the Arruda brothers. Two examples are the window openings on a central line in the façades, and the knots in the ropes marking the various floors horizontally on the outside, also on a central line and in vertical alignment.

Left Image in stone of Saint Vincent on the north-east corner of the tower; Saint Vincent was the patron saint of Lisbon.

Above Large gallery or loggia of the Tower. This is the most palatial feature, which contrasts with the military austerity of the bastion. It stands on a row of modillions, evoking machicolations.

Opposite Battlement with the Cross of Christ. The pavises, or stone shields, would have been an allusion to the great ship that used to be anchored in the river and which, before the Tower was built, was the means of defence for the entrance of the Tagus, in combination with artillery from the Torre Velha.

THE WORK OF BROTHERS DIOGO AND FRANCISCO DE ARRUDA

At this point it is worth remembering the constructions of the Arruda brothers (Diogo, the elder, and Francisco, author of the design of the tower) which finally gave a uniquely national flavour to the Mediterranean and Nordic characteristics of late Gothic architecture in Portugal. They both contributed to the creation of their own style, which is easily characterised: the systematic use of cylindrical shapes; the use of military rhetoric as a form of architectural iconology; the loading or masking of their works with hyperrealist decoration, based on references to the world of nature or the world of man-made objects (from roots and leaves to heraldry).

Left Detail of the Torre de Belém: cornice with "Manueline" knot.

Below General view of the Palace of Evoramonte (Diogo and Francisco de Arruda, c. 1530).

The case of Diogo is particularly interesting, since, according to Rafael Moreira's hypothesis, he may possibly have served his apprenticeship on military architecture projects on the Italian peninsula, according to possible evidence relating to constructions in the kingdom. 'An unusual case, and worthy of careful consideration, is that of "Maestro Diego portoghese" who in 1485-1486 was in the service of Alfonso II of Aragon, Duke of Calabria, together with two other Italian engineers (none other than Baccio Pontelli and Francesco di Giorgio Martini), remodelling the outer wall of Naples and building coastal fortifications against the Turks in Apulia (Taranto, Brindisi, Gallipoli). We think this refers to Diogo de Arruda, who died an old man in 1531 and would at that time have been around 30. This would perfectly explain the early and direct influence of Francesco di Giorgio Martini on the work of the Arruda brothers, especially when applied to buildings motivated by military imperatives – if not by urgent military need.

The oldest construction in which the intervention of one of the Arruda brothers – in this case Diogo de Arruda – is recorded is the bastion of the palace of Ribeira, a fortified tower with watchtowers at either end, already distinctive for the remarkable dimension of royal heraldry.

Later Diogo went to Tomar, where he was partially responsible for the new Manueline choir and built the spectacular western window, in which are synthesized practically all the ornamen-

Above Detail of the spiral staircase giving access to the different floors of the tower.

Opposite Detail of the side of the tower.

tal motifs that are an original feature of many of his constructions (royal heraldry, plant symbolism). In 1510 he worked as a military engineer in Azamor, and returned from North Africa a short time later.

In his turn, Francisco was commissioned to repair the fortifications of Moura, Mourão and Portel, where his most significant intervention was to be found. There, as well as repairing the walls, he added to the castle semicircular towers which are already distinctive for their transitional style, reflecting the changes wrought by developments in artillery. He built for Dom Jaime, Duke of Bragança, the palaces of the castle of Portel, today ruined, and the chapel of São João Baptista, also badly deteriorated: this had two voluminous buttresses on its straight front wall, cylindrical at the base and octagonal towards the top, crowned by twisted conical pinnacles preceded by a rope moulding (a combination of forms identical to the choir at Tomar).

Diogo returned to North Africa, to Safim and Mazagão, accompanied by Francisco, who also worked on the stronghold of Azamor. At Safim he built the monumental bastion of São Cristovão, which used building principles designed for static defence – powerful cannon apertures and towers with a large operational diameter; while at Azamor he built the bastion of Raio, which is further testament to the monumental preferences of the Arruda brothers, with its curved wall and the application of large and persuasive heraldic iconography. In 1518 Diogo directed the Castelo Novo project in Évora, an original construction with a broad central courtyard and four parallelepiped towers at the corners. Much transformed today, the castle originally had battlements all the way round and a thicker base, as well as three round watchtowers, similar to the palace of Ribeira.

Diogo de Arruda's involvement is also documented in the convent of Santa Clara at Estremoz and in the monastery of Espinheiro in 1520, and around that time he was also appointed master of royal works in the Alentejo and Royal Surveyor, working with his brother Francisco on several projects in Évora and the surrounding area, notably the monastery of São Francisco. He went on in 1525 to remodel the royal palace at Évora, strongly inspired by the palace of Ribeira, with the Galeria das Damas or Ladies' Gallery on a continuous porch with a tower in the middle, a rhetorical reminder of the military defence systems in which he specialised. The plan of the Sé or cathedral of Elvas, which shares a characteristic design with the Igreja Matriz (mother church) of Olivença, with its large central tower, can also be attributed to Francisco de Arruda during this period.

Leaving aside the interventions that show an already advanced Renaissance reading of military architecture, the building of the fortress of Evoramonte (begun in 1531 at the behest of the Duke of Bragança) is of particular importance. With its quadrangular central plan, and with sub-cylindrical towers at the corners, it corresponds to an 'ideal' vision of military architecture. This was a military construction, but it was also a hunting lodge. The iconography that decorates the three floors of this imposing and solid-looking building uses the themes of flames and cannonballs to accentuate its artillery function, features already observed in the Torre de Belém. The form adopted clearly reflects the influence of the most prestigious building of its kind that had been built in Europe up to that time, the château of Chambord, whose central block has cylindrical towers at the corners (although on a much larger scale). The actual military function of Evoramonte does not conceal its status as an 'imaginary' castle, still harking back to a chivalric and romantic conception of the role of the nobility. This trend is further evidenced in the 1530s by the rise in popularity of epic literature deriving from medieval exploits and the tales of the Holy Grail, such as for example the famous *Palmeirim de Inglaterra* by Francisco de Morais, in which, curiously, the fortress of the giant Califúrnio is inspired by Chambord, for Morais was author of the earliest description of the French château, which he visited when ambassador. At Evoramente the usual decorative devices of the Arruda brothers are displayed in a purified form; the vertical central lines of the façades feature windows beneath which we find the usual knots, in this case, the emblem of Dom Jaime. It is also said that the design of the palace may even reflect the suggestions of cylindrical volumes in the fifteenth-century designs of Francesco di Giorgio Martini.

Diogo de Arruda died in 1531 and his brother Francisco then gradually followed a different path, converting little by little to humanism. Francisco's subsequent work begins to show signs of Renaissance (or early Renaissance) erudition. Two examples, both attributed to him, are the Casa dos Bicos in Lisbon, where an attachment to the Mudéjar form can again be noted and the façade is organised with contrasting surfaces (the magnificent loggia with three bays, today reconstructed), and the remarkable Bacalhoa palace, in its initial phase (1530?), which has two large cylindrical towers topped with parachute domes.

Thus the architecture of the Arruda brothers contains the fundamental ingredients of the Manueline style: on the one hand, the taste for clear volumes well-defined in overall design terms; on the other hand, the highlighting of the architecture by the application of intricate ornamentation, often more popular than erudite in nature, either fairly immediate echoes of the function of the building or simply the direct result of granting unprecedented freedom to the carvers, who then translated the potentialities of a new iconic discourse onto the edges of the constructions, so that it rivalled the emblematic nature of state or formal discourse.

THE TOWER INTERIOR

On the first floor of the tower is the *Sala do Governador* or Governor's Room, with a central well supplied by a tank. This room was undoubtedly functional, being used for customs inspection and the collection of various taxes, as it is on the same level as the bastioned terrace.

Console with 'leaf mask'.

A spiral staircase communicates with the upper floors, and its volume is visible on the outside of the tower.

Immediately above is the *Sala dos Reis* or Kings' Hall, with a fireplace built obliquely into the wall. It is roofed with a groin vault skilfully constructed and profiled to absorb the spandrels created by the opening of the embrasures leading to the exterior balconies. It is, without doubt, the most noble room in the tower, with direct access to the long narrow veranda or loggia and to the three bay windows or balconies. Here will be found greater evidence of the stately nature of the building, evidenced both in the relative comfort of the room, and above all in its overall festive and ornamented character.

Above this is the so-called *Sala das Audiências* or Assembly Room, also with a groin vault, and benches facing one another by the paired windows.

The last room, with full-length seats, is the richest in strictly architectural terms. It has a rib vaulting with keystones decorated with royal heraldry. The ribs spring from corbels, two of them paired and with unusual ornamentation, notably with 'flames' and a grotesque figure which is similar to the green-man or 'leaf mask' design that symbolises Time. Also known as the chapel, this room has a floor in a black and white chequerboard pattern and,

Opposite Upper room or chapel. Note the stone ribbed vault.

Below Kings' room. The noble room par excellence, although not the most complete in architectural terms, it reveals a luxurious character similar to a belvedere, since it gives access to the loggia and the side verandas.

Above Upper room; detail of the decoration of the keystones of the vault with royal heraldic motifs and the chequerboard floor.

Right Governor's room; this is the room you enter directly from the terrace of the bastion. It is roofed by a groin vault with access to the sentry posts or watchtowers at the corners. The outlet of the water tank serving the tower is here.

Opposite Detail of one of the Mudéjar capitals, called 'turban', that appear on the verandas and galleries.

Above Kings' room; showing
the fireplace and the
chequerboard floor.

Right Console with 'flame'
decoration.

Opposite Upper room, known
as the "chapel": vault keystone
with the Cross of Christ

in the centre, a white octagon containing a black rectangle which has given rise to esoteric readings, given its peculiar combination of symbols.

THE ARMILLARY SPHERE

In the Torre de Belém, more than in any other Manueline monument, heraldry plays a clear role. The general importance of this role had grown continuously since the fifteenth century, as the court exhibited a liking for its rhetorical efficacy as a representation of power and a distinctive sign of the nobility, and this was further emphasised by Dom Manuel, who was particularly keen to entrench the kingdom and the legitimacy of his royal lineage. It could even be argued that this monarch gave the discipline of heraldry unprecedented relevance, but it could already be foreseen in the times of Dom Afonso V and in many of the courtly celebrations of Dom João II's time. Indeed, some Manueline buildings stand as authentic altars to personality and to individualism. The use of heraldry was extended to all structures.

It is evident that this cult of personality in the times of Dom Manuel had other referents, related to the political doctrine of the period, whether these were imperial in nature, related to family, or even simply ritualised on the occasion of festivals and celebrations. Totally steeped in this emblematic culture from early on, Dom Manuel participated in the celebrations of the marriage of Infante Dom Afonso to the daughter of the Catholic Monarchs of Spain in November 1490 in Évora, bringing 'seven jousters with the seven planets' and with himself as the 'God Saturn', showing an inclination towards the symbolic which was to become accentuated through the use of his personal emblem, the armillary sphere. Used since the time when he was still Duke of Beja, this emblem was bestowed on him by the king, Dom João II, himself. But its symbolism took on greater significance when it was interpreted *a posteriori* as a sign of his royal destiny, 'which appeared mysterious and prophetic because it gave him hope of his royal succession', according to Garcia de Resende. Damião de Góis goes on to explain the rationale of Dom Manuel's adoption of the 'figure of Hope, because mathematicians represent the form of the whole machinery of the sky and earth and all the other elements (...) because as it was ordained by God that he was to be heir to King Dom João II so he wished that the King himself, whom he was to succeed, would bestow on him such an emblem which would demonstrate the handing over and transfer that he was now making to him as his heir to continue after his death in the true manifestation that was his in the conquest and dominion of Asia and Africa as he did with much praise and honour of these kingdoms'.

Scattered around on all the buildings built at royal behest (and on all Manueline documents and certificates), the armillary sphere became not only the symbol of the king but, systematically associated with the Cross of Christ and the Royal Shield, the symbol of the very empire. As regards its duality (or perhaps its dual validity), Ana Maria Alves has already dedicated an exemplary study to this. Almost always appearing in dual form on the pediments and portals of important buildings or on the title pages of chronicles and state books, this duality relates to its Aristotelian nature by representing simultaneously Heaven and Earth. It is on the one hand a personal symbol and on the other a symbol of State; and it becomes an allegory for royal power in the kingdom and in the empire. Indeed, interpretation of the Manueline motto allows for a duplication of meanings, combining the hope (*espera*) of the world (in the sense of the conquests and the expansion of Christianity) with the sphere (*esfera*) of the world (in the cosmological sense).

Its eminently 'abstract' nature demonstrates the power of the king to his subjects but at the same time separates him from them. It is also evident that this symbol represents perfection – the perfection expressed by the sphere as a pure form. And this came to be seen as upholding one of the great dogmas of Manueline politics: the divine right of royal power. Emanating from the anointing of King David, the conception of royal power as providential found its Manueline expression in the work *De Republica Gubernanda per Regem*, by Diogo

Opposite Terrace.

Below Detail of one of the armillary spheres decorating the Tower.

de Lopes Rebelo, who was master of grammar to Dom Manuel when he was still Duke of Beja. This book, printed in Paris in 1496, clearly champions the divine right of kings, since the power held by the monarch is conferred upon him by God, making him lord over the life and death of men, as Moreira de Sá points out. This is merely confirmation of the existence of a political doctrine to which Dom Manuel visibly subscribed, and in which imagert played a primordial role.

It is not by chance that the armillary sphere is represented in duplicate on the frontispieces of illuminated books, sometimes supported by putti, and on either side of two angels holding the royal shield against a background divided into white and crimson (the heraldic colours of Dom Manuel), or on a sky swathed in clouds (as in the copy of a chronicle, with the city of Lisbon, worldly seat of the empire, at the bottom).

And so it was that the Torre de Belém assumed the role of frontispiece to Lisbon itself – and to the kingdom.

In its established function as 'entrance' to the kingdom, the invocation of the Torre de Belém, dedicated to Saint Vincent, also played an important role. Indeed, at the gates to the city, the first and most imposing building that came into view was protected by this saint. But this sign has to be read in conjunction with other signs, such as the invocation of the Torre Velha, which is dedicated to Saint Sebastian and the patron saint of the 'great ship', Saint Christopher. Pedro Cid explains this fact, which was clearly not the product of chance: 'Saint Vincent was the patron saint of Lisbon, in whose cathedral was an urn containing his mortal remains, while Saint Sebastian was considered at the time the best ally against contagious diseases, which were seen as "darts from God" (which would not kill, just as the arrows of the Roman soldiers had not killed him). It should be noted that both saints were put to death on the orders of the same emperor, Diocletian. As for Saint Christopher, he was the giant who protected both travellers and professions such as harquebusiers (...).'

What we have here is a manifestation of the Christian miracles, and even of sacred principles in an – at least apparently – strictly military context.

THE ARCHITECTURAL SIGNIFICANCE

The architectural significance of the Torre de Belém cannot and should not be measured in strictly military terms.

Indeed, historical records show that the Tower was in the end of little use in its own time – the sixteenth century – in preventing fleets from penetrating the entrance of the Tagus, and this was even more true in the seventeenth and nineteenth centuries, although its unusual form and its grandeur will have served to dissuade many aggressive actions. The construction of the large and innovative Fortress of São Julião da Barra, under the direction of Miguel de Arruda from 1552 onwards, which was called by many 'the shield of the kingdom' and was long and modern and terribly imposing, with its batteries of artillery, is evidence that a need continued to be felt to strengthen coastal vigilance in the area around the entrance to the Tagus.

It is above all in the domain of architectural invention that the Torre de Belém has become famous. In the middle of the nineteenth century the cultural context of Romanticism in Europe as a whole inspired among the intellectual elite an interest in the medieval past and in the age of the discoveries. Patterns of taste changed drastically and medieval architecture became an object of study. The same thing happened in Portugal with the architecture of Dom Manuel's time. In fact, it was around 1842 that the designation 'Manueline architecture' was coined, and has been understood since then to be a typically Portuguese 'style'. It was the Jerónimos

Opposite left Neo-Manueline Romantic revivalism: the Porta do Ferro or monumental gateway of Pena Palace, reproducing the watchtowers of the Torre de Belém, according to a drawing by D. Fernando II (c. 1842/1848), covered with the protruding diamond design characteristic of the Casa dos Bicos, in an allusion to the Portuguese maritime discoveries.

Opposite right Detail of drawing of the watchtower which was to adorn the elevation of the gateway

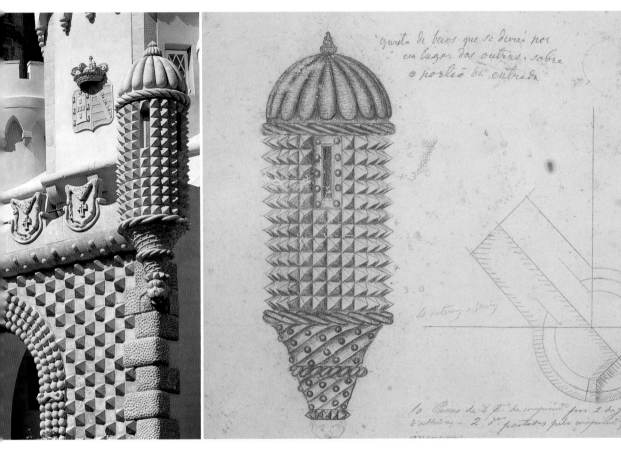

monastery that gave rise to this designation and it was that building that became the paradigm of the so-called 'style of the maritime discoveries', but its neighbour, the Torre de Belém, also attracted similar attention.

It was, even then, the first monument visible at the approach to Lisbon and it gallantly displayed its impressive form, in spite of being put to a number of inappropriate uses (as a barracks and as the base for a lighthouse) over the years. It was therefore a natural development that the Torre de Belém, the Manueline monument par excellence – located moreover in a privileged position in terms of visibility – became a leading light in the context of Romantic revivalism.

The first, and highly significant, sign of what we might call 'Torre-de-Belém-mania' can be seen in the construction of the monumental gateway to the magnificent Pena Palace, one of the first and most complete and complex architectural constructions of European revivalism. Watchtowers similar to those of the Torre de Belém were placed at either side of the entrance. This monumental gateway was augmented in around 1833-1834 and the original gate combined with the drawbridge. Various versions of the watchtowers were drawn, with one of them used as the final model. The drawings are not signed but are certainly attributable to Dom Fernando II, and it can be seen that the inclusion of these structures was to fulfil a specific wish of the king, as we have indicated elsewhere. On the drawing that was used for the building of the watchtowers, Dom Fernando left a note instructing the master builders to construct them as we see them today, 'instead of the others'. They are juxtaposed, with great visibility and evocative power, to the palace entrance, with parachute domes (interpreted at the time as a theme of Indian origin) and the familiar enveloping rope, although composed in a

Above Torre de Belém and beach, early twentieth century. Photograph by Paulo Guedes (Arquivo Fotográfico de Lisboa, CML)

Opposite above Torre de Belém, coast road and the Belém Gasworks, 1912. Photograph by Joshua Benoliel. (Arquivo Fotográfico de Lisboa, CML)

Opposite Torre de Belém, with a lighthouse built on the terrace. In the background you can see the silhouette of the Belém Gasworks, early twentieth century. Photograph by Paulo Guedes. (Arquivo Fotográfico de Lisboa, CML)

hybrid form with a surface inspired by the 'diamond-point' decoration of the Casa dos Bicos in Lisbon. They were, of course, a reference to the Portuguese discoveries. We also see, in the tower commissioned by Fernando II and designed by Baron de Eschwege at Pena Palace, another allusion to the Torre de Belém, in the arrangement of the cylindrical watch-towers, which serve – highly romantically – as its crowning ornament.

Another example of the tower's architectural influence, among many others scattered around the country in minor architectural references, can be found at the sumptuous Palace Hotel in Buçaco, built in the early twentieth century. It is the work of Italian architect and set designer Luigi Manini, an enthusiast for Manueline art, who summarised in it practically all the buildings that had by then come to be seen as Portugal's architectural heritage – all of them Manueline. The tower of the Palace Hotel makes an immediate reference to the Torre de Belém, but the way the structures are arranged, with the main residential building at the bottom and a terrace above looked over by the tower, also evokes the layout of the structures of the Torre de Belém. In addition, all the ornamentation derives from various Manueline examples, with the Jerónimos monastery serving as the main model, and including the Torre de Belém.

The fever even led to a scale replica of the Torre de Belém being built in the twentieth century in São Vicente, one of the Cape Verde Islands. Situated by the sea in the capital Mindelo, it is open to the public.

The consequence of this 'Torre-de-Belém-mania' can be seen in the unprecedented profusion of souvenirs and miniature replicas of the building that were – and still are – produced. Versions made from pastry, models built of matches and cork, key-rings (with the Torre de Belem in three-dimensions, in cross-section or relief); plastic kits, pop-out books, cardboard cut-out construction kits; models made of copper or bronze, used as paperweights or purely as ornaments; they come in practically every possible version you can think of.

It has become widely known as a prestigious monument and has been listed as a World Heritage Site by UNESCO since 1983, and modern media technology is taking this into new realms. It has been used countless times as a setting – but only as a backdrop – for launching all manner of products, notably, of course, those of the motor industry. As an illustration of Lisbon, it has become a metonym for the image of the city and as such is equivalent to the Eiffel Tower, the Empire State Building or the Colosseum in Rome, being a member of that very special club – the most select imaginable – of great landmarks which of themselves symbolise Europe.

Above left Demolition of the chimneys of the Gasworks, c. 1950. (Arquivo Fotográfico de Lisboa, CML)

Above Torre de Belém, with Tagus caïque in the foreground. c. 1930 (?). Photograph by Ferreira da Cunha (Arquivo Fotográfico de Lisboa, CML)

Opposite Copy of the Torre de Belém, port authority headquarters in the town of Mindelo (Republic of Cape Verde), in the 1920s.

SELECTED BIBLIOGRAPHY

Aa.vv., *História das Artes Plásticas*, Lisbon, IN–CM, Európália 91, 1991.

ALBUQUERQUE, Martim de, *O poder político no Renascimento português*, Lisbon, 1968.

ALVES, Ana Maria, *Iconologia do Poder Real no Período Manuelino*, Lisbon, IN–CM, 1985.

ALVES, Ana Maria, *As Entradas Régias Portuguesas*, Lisbon, Horizonte, not dated.

ALVES, José da Felicidade, *O Mosteiro dos Jerónimos*, vol.I, Lisbon, Horizonte, 1989.

ANDERSON, William, *Green Man*, London, Harper Collins, 1990.

ATANAZIO, M. C. Mendes, *A Arte do Manuelino*, Lisbon, Presença, 1984.

ATANAZIO, M. C. Mendes, *Arquitectura do Manuelino. Novos problemas de espaço e técnica*, Moçâmedes, 1969.

AVERINI, Ricardo, "Sul Manuelino" in *Colóquio Artes*, 2nd series, no 56, Mar. 1983.

BARREIRA, João, *Arte portuguesa. Evolução estética*, Lisbon, Exselsior, not dated.

BARROCA, Mário J., "Em torno da residência senhorial fortificada. Quatro torres medievais da região de Amares", *Revista de História*, vol.IX, Porto, 1989.

BARROCA, Mário J., "Os Castelos" in *Nos Confins da Idade Média* (dir. Luis Adão da Fonseca), exhibition catalogue, Brussels, Európália 91, 1991.

BARROS, João de, *Décadas da Ásia*, I, Coimbra, 1932.

BARROS, João de, *Panegíricos*, Lisbon, Sá da Costa, 2nd ed., 1943.

BARROS, João de, *Crónica do Imperador Clarimundo*, 2 vols., Lisbon, Sá da Costa, 1953.

BASCAPÉ, Giancomo, DEL PIAZZO, Marcello del, *Insigni e Simboli. Araldica Pubblica e Privata medieval e moderna*, Rome, 1983.

BASSANI, Ezio and William Fagg, *Africa and the Renaissance. Art in Ivory*, New York, 1988.

Batisseurs des Cathédrales Gothiques (Les) (dir. Roland Recht), exhibition catalogue, Strasbourg, Les musées de la ville de Strasbourg, 1989.

BERTAUX, Emile, "Les Arts en Portugal" in *Les Guides Bleus. Portugal, Madeira – Açores*, Paris, Hachette, 1935.

BERTAUX, Emile, *La renaissance en Espagne et au Portugal in Histoire de l'Art* (dir. André Michel), vol. IV, Paris, Armand Colin, 1911.

BIALOSTOCKI, Jan, "Le gothique tardif: désacords sur le concept" in *L'Information d'histoire de l'art*, no 3, 1968, pp. 10–128.

BRANDI, Cesare, "Il Manuelino" in *Struttura e Architettura*, Turin, Einaudi, 2nd ed. 1971, pp. 301–307.

CAAMAÑO, Jesus Maria, "Conexiones entre el hispanoflamenco y el manuelino" in *As relações artísticas entre Portugal e Espanha na Época dos Descobrimentos* (dir. Pedro Dias), Coimbra, Minerva, 1987.

Cancioneiro Geral de Garcia de Resende, (5 vols. prefaces and notes by Andrée Crabé Rocha), Centro do Livro Brasileiro, 1973.

CID, Pedro Aboim, Inglez, *A Torre de São Sebstião a Caparica e a arquitectura militar do tempo de D. João II*, Lisbon, UNL, FCSH, Master's thesis dissertation, 1998.

CID, Pedro Aboim, Inglez, "As arquitecturas a barra do Tejo: as fortificações" in *Nossa Senhora dos Mártires. A última viagem*, Lisbon, Expo 98, 1998, pp. 32–49.

CORDEIRO, *Luciano, Uma sobrinha do Infante Imperatriz da Allemanha e Rainha da Hungria*, Lisbon, Imp. Nac., 1894.

CORREIA, Vergílio, *As obras de Santa Maria de Belém* 1514 a 1519, Lisbon, 1922.

CORREIA, Vergílio, "Arte: ciclo manuelino" in *História de Portugal* (Barcelos), vol. IV, Portucalense Editora, 1933, pp. 433–474.

CORREIA, Vergílio, *Três cidades de Marrocos. Azemôr, Mazagão, Çafim*, 2nd ed., Porto, ed. Manuel Barreira, not dated.

D'ARMAS, D., *Livro das Fortalezas* (reprod. annotated by João de Almeida), Lisbon, 1943.

DESWARTE, Sylvie, *Les Enluminures de la "Leitura Nova"* 1504–1522, Paris, Fundação Calouste Gulbenkian, 1977.

DIAS, Pedro, "A Igreja do Convento de Jesus na evolução da Arquitectura do Manuelino" in *Belas Artes*, 2nd series, no 32, 1978.

DIAS, Pedro, "O Mudejarismo na Arte Coimbrã" in *Arquivo Coimbrão*, vol. XXVII, 1979.

DIAS, Pedro, *Visitações da Ordem de Cristo de 1507 a 1510. Aspectos artísticos*, Coimbra, 1979.

DIAS, Pedro, *A arquitectura de Coimbra na transição do gótico para a renascença*, 1490–1540, Coimbra, 1982.

DIAS, Pedro, "A Arquitectura do Gótico final e a decoração Manuelina" in *O Manuelino* (vol. 5, of the História de Arte em Portugal), Lisbon, Publicações Alfa, 1986, pp. 7–91.

DIAS, Pedro, *A Arquitectura Manuelina*, Porto, 1988.

EVIN, Paul A., *L' Architecture Portugaise au Maroc et le Style Manuélin*, Lisbon, Institut Français au Portugal, 1942.

EVIN, Paul A., *Étude sur le style manuélin*, Paris, 1948.

EVIN, Paul A., "Style manuelin et Spatgotik: les critiques du symbolisme maritime" in *Ciência e Trópico*, No. 2, vol. 13, 1985.

EVIN, Paul A., "Faut-il voir un symbolisme maritime dans la décoration Manueline?", in *Acte du Congrès International d'Histoire de l'Art*, vol. 2, 1949, pp. 191–198.

FERREIRA DE ALMEIDA, Carlos Alberto, *Barcelos*, Lisbon, Presença, 1990.

FIGUEIREDO, Fidelino de, A Épica Portuguesa no Século XVI (facsimile ed. of the 1950 ed.), Lisbon, IN–CM, 1987.

FRANCO, Anísio (dir.), *Jerónimos. 4 Séculos de Pintura*, exhibition catalogue, Lisbon, IPPC, 1992.

GARCIA MERCADAL, J., *Viajes de extranjeros por España y Portugal*, Madrid, Aguilar, 1952.

GOIS, Damião de, *Crónica do Felicíssimo Rei D. Manuel*, 4 vols., Coimbra, Imp. da Univ., 1949–1954.

GOIS, Damião de, *Descrição da Cidade de Lisboa*, Lisbon, Horizonte, 1988.

GUILLAUME, Jean and Rafael Moreira, "La première description de Chambord", *Revue de l'Art*, CNRS, 1988.

HAUPT, Albrecht, *A Arquitectura do Renascimento em Portugal* (critical introduction by M. C. Mendes Atanázio), Lisbon, Presença, 1986.

HERCULANO, Alexandre, "Viagem dos Cavaleiros Tron e Lippomani. 1580 in *Opúsculos*, 2nd vol. VI, Lisbon, 1897.

Hospital Real de Todos-os-Santos, exhibition catalogue, Lisbon, CML, 1993.

LEITE, Ana Cristina, PEREIRA, Paulo, "Para uma leitura da simbólica manuelina", in Prelo, no 5, Oct.–Dec. 1984, pp. 51–74.

MARIAS, Fernando, *El Largo Siglo XVI*, Madrid, Taurus, 1989.

MORAIS, Francisco de, *Palmeirim de Inglaterra* (selection, discussions, prefaces and notes by Rodrigues Lapa), Lisbon, Textos Literários, 2nd ed. 1960.

MOREIRA, Rafael, "A arquitectura militar do Renascimento em Portugal" in *Actas do Simpósio sobre a introdução da arte da Renascença na Peninsula Ibérica*, Coimbra, Epartur, 1981, pp. 281–305.

MOREIRA, Rafael, "Arquitectura" in *Catálogo da XVII Exposição de Arte Ciência e Cultura do Conselho da Europa, Arte Antiga – I*, Lisbon, 1983, pp. 307–352.

MOREIRA, Rafael, *Jerónimos*, Lisbon, Verbo, 1987.

MOREIRA, Rafael, *A Arquitectura do Renascimento no Sul de Portugal*, Lisbon, 1991.

MOREIRA, Rafael, *A Arquitectura Militar na Expansão Portuguesa*, Porto, CNCDP, 1994.

MOREIRA, Rafael, "Santa Maria de Belém" in *O Livro de Lisboa*, Lisbon, Lisboa 94/Horizonte, 1994.

MOREIRA, Rafael, "A Torre de Belém" in *O Livro de Lisboa*, Lisbon, Lisboa 94/Horizonte, 1994.

PAIS DA SILVA, J. H, *Páginas de História* de Arte, 2 vols., Lisbon, Estampa, 1986.

PEREIRA, Paulo, *Evoramonte. A Fortaleza*, Lisbon, IPPC, 1989.

PEREIRA, Paulo, *A Obra Silvestre e a Esfera do Rei*, Coimbra, Universidade de Coimbra, 1990.

PEREIRA, Paulo, "Architecture manuéline: thèmes et problèmes de méthode" in A *Travers l'Image*, Paris, Klinksieck/CNRS, 1993a.

PEREZ EMBID, Florentino, El *Mudejarismo en la Arquitectura Portuguesa de la Época Manuelina*, Seville, 1944.

RESENDE, Garcia de, *Crónica de D.João II e Miscelânea* (with an introduction by Joaquim Verissímo Serrão), Lisbon, IN–CM, 1973.

SANTOS, Reinaldo dos, *A Torre de Belém*, Coimbra, Imp. da Univ., 1922.

SANTOS, Reinaldo dos, *O Estilo Manuelino*, Lisbon, 1952.

SARAIVA, José Hermano, *Ditos portugueses dignos de memória*, Lisbon, not dated.

VARNHAGEN, Francisco Adolfo, *Notícia Histórica e Descriptiva do Mosteiro de Belém*, Lisbon, 1842.

VIEIRA DA SILVA, José Custódio, *O tardo-gótico na arquitectura. A arquitectura religiosa do Alto Alentejo*, Lisbon, Horizonte, 1989.

VITERBO, F. Sousa, *Dicionário Histórico e documental dos architectos, engenheiros e construtores portuguezes ou ao serviço de Portugal*, 3 vols., Lisbon, (1899–1922), facsimile ed., Lisbon IN–CM, 1988.

INDEX